UNDER YOUR NAILS

Under Your Nails

Poems of Love,
Loss, and Healing

Lauren Marelli

Cover design by Euan Monaghan
Editing by Sage Taylor Kingsley www.SageforYourPage.com
ISBN: 979-8-218-56869-6
First Edition

Published by Lauren Marelli
Contact: laurenmarelli.writer@gmail.com

For those who need to know
others feel it too

Contents

Red

I want a rose—
a foolish declaration of love.
I want a rose so red that,
should I crush it in my hand,
the petals,
mangled and bruised,
would seep and stain my fingers
a bloody crimson.

Uncaring

You paid no attention to my heart
as it latched itself onto you
with such devotion,
such mighty optimism.

No Finer Meal

He asked if he could eat me—
devour me with knife and fork,
upon plate of fine china,
as nine figures flanked him.

Women he could no longer sense –
wispy, floating echoes
of what were,
now gone from this plane.

I looked to them for the answer
as he waited for mine,
because I did not know
which would save me.

With eyes devoid of light,
chins tipped down,
lips curled,

When they nodded,
so did I.

When he grinned,
so did I.

Little Ghost

He named me something new
to match my state of being,
formed by his influence,

a fitting name
for one who vanishes in his shadow,
unseen but always there,

who lingers over his shoulder,
whose wails and moans
find only his ear,

whose chill
from a long-dead soul
tingles down his spine.

A name that broke me ...
until his shell began to crack,
and I accepted myself
as the one who haunts him.

Beside Me

I like his cries in the night
and that he doesn't know he makes them.

I like that if I stay awake after sleep has claimed him,
I see the raw world he hides from me.

I like that, in this world, he whimpers my name
as if I am out of reach,

and sobs for my affection
as if he does not have it.

I like that his heart wholly desires
what only my heart can give.

So, desperate as I am,
I do not like when he wakes up.

Under Your Nails

It was not I who cracked my chest
and peeled myself apart for you.
I did not vandalize tissue
or carelessly break bone.

You pried me open with bitter fingers
and gritted teeth.
Bits of me are forever trapped
under your nails.

Shifter

I did not think I would love you.
Our tattoos did not match,
your knuckles pushed mine too far apart,
the width of your hips brought an ache
to my thighs.

As the seasons turned beneath our tangled limbs
I drew Sharpie lines on my skin
and got used to the cramps in my fingers.
My muscles stretched so my legs
could spread wider.

We fit then,
complemented one another
after all my hard work.
Patiently I am waiting to see
how you will shapeshift for me.

Dancing Darling

I watch you in slow motion
under throbbing lights of color
that alter the shade of your skin.
The thumps of hearts echo
the beats that fill the room.

You dance for me
as you grab her hips
and pull her against you,
grinding through fabric layers.

One misspoken word from my lips
has you abandoning me for another,
showing what I could lose at any given moment,
and what awaits you
if I am gone.

Breakdown

A frail, glass box—
that is all that contains my madness.

But I threw a pebble at it
and now the cracks are growing;
the flood of my emotions
spewing through thin, jagged spaces,
the pressure
threatening its walls.

And they will shatter
because that is what they do.

The lid will cave
and disaster will coat the floor

beneath my feet.

For Now

When I touch my lips to yours
for the first time in months,
I whimper—
whimper and melt,
and the tears want to come,
because it is much easier to resist desire
if one has not entertained it
in a while.

But I have given in.
I am tasting you like I used to:
remnants of gin and cigarettes
and blueberry pie,
and it is all *you*.

You,
who are so shocked by my kiss
that it takes you a moment to catch up
and become the you that I know.

But you find me,
and then I am in your lap,
hands everywhere –
thighs, spine, holding the back of my head –
tongue in mouth, teeth nipping lips,
and I have decided
I shall not deprive myself of you
again.

At least...
not until you hurt me
once more.

Illness

Can you love too fiercely?
Too aggressively?
Can you love like a plague?
> *I would love to be sick.*

Will you love the way I love,
so I will not be disappointed?

Will you let my love
take you down with me,
and accept what you have denied?
> *We are meant to be.*

Devour

Devour me whole
in the way that you do.
Eat me alive, and believe me,
I'll let you.

Trouble

I do not search for Trouble.
Trouble comes for me.
When on bended knee I begged for peace,
Trouble whispered back:
Not a chance.

By Your Hand

I do not fear the end of life,
but rather the torture
that precedes it.

Hellbound

I hurt you in ways I should not,
with verbs and adjectives
and lack of truth;
cleaving apart your goodness,
your kindness,
your gentle disposition,
to pull a demon from your core,
so we can match, equal,
the same.

Drop-Off

In the abyss—
in the fog that caresses the sea—
my body is beckoned forth
by each weighty, wild wave
that crashes against uneven rock
hidden in the ghostly haze.

It is all dark—
sun suffocated above the black deep,
and now I stand higher,
on cliffs sturdy to the wintry winds.

Chilled to the core—
frozen,
but I could be colder still.

Broken

Sad
as I am,
sick
as I am,
weak
as I am,
I still love the one
who breaks me.

Spinning Top

We spin so smoothly
on our descent into disaster,
even and mesmerizing.
We hypnotically witness
as we wait in the silence
of our pending collapse;
the inevitable catastrophe
of our
downfall.

Inflexible

What do we do if the last petal falls
and neither of us bends our backs
to catch it?

Should it touch the ground,
Earth will reclaim it
to grow anew
on another couple's flower.

Shriveled stem,
rotten roots,
will be all that is left
of us.

Oxygen

They decided breathing
was the hardest part
of being together;
the filling of lungs
despite the boulders
they placed upon one another's chests.

The Handyman

You
do not get
to take me apart
simply because
you are
bored
if you do not bother
to put me back
together
once you are done.

Picnic

I will lie among the dead,
checkered blanket spread wide
between their headstones,
and on my back, we will face the sky together,
and on my back, I will tell them what I see,
marvel at formations of birds in flight,
laugh at the living who walk by
with lifted brows,
point out shapes of clouds
even as they turn gray,
stay while released raindrops hit our skin
and drench the soil,
loosening it so we sink to skeleton sides,
to remain until Earth solidifies
under unshielded sun.

I Followed

I followed him
as he crooked his finger,
beckoning for my trailing behind.

I followed into the woods,
tripping over logs he walked through,
leaves crunching under my boots—

his bare feet
did not crunch;
neither did they bleed
from the sharp points of dry leaves.

Not once did he look over his shoulder;
he knew what I was abandoning.

I followed into the water,
ripple-less from his descending form,
and sank with the stone
he tied around my ankle.

The world shifted season
as breath was lost,
and I pointed my finger toward the sky
to crack the underbelly of the frozen lake.
But I could not,
before I met my muddy bed
and slept.

Lessons

I learned to kiss from porn,
learned to moan from porn,
learned how to contort my body,
learned to praise men the way men were praised
on my small screen—
without questioning the worthiness of that praise.

Do they do it well?
I see no reason to think about it.
I know I do it well.
They make the sounds they are supposed to make,
fill me as they are meant to.
They do not check my satisfaction,
but I have been taught not to care.

So I do not feel robbed,
I do not feel the unfairness in the tainted air.
I do my job,
they are satisfied,
and my mind says that is all
that matters.

Are You Here?

How odd
to crave the sound of breathing;
to ache for silent inhales,
quieter exhales;
to listen for a whisper of breath;
desperate
for a cheek to flush a lively shade
under the influence of my fingertip;
to feel a pulse rush under a jaw
from the soft press of my lips.
How spoiled I was
by the reactions I expected to receive
without a fuss,
only to learn,
under the threat of absence,
they were never guaranteed.

Terrors

I grew, I aged, I became,
and yet,
I never stopped sleeping
as poorly as I did
when I believed in the monster
under my bed.

Lost

I draw faces in the spaces in the walls
where periwinkle paint has chipped
to reveal pale plaster.

These snaggy patches contain within them
forms of crooked nose, of pointy chin,
of outturned ears.

Twelve there are now—friends—
some winking, some laughing, some screaming
at the fate of being trapped in cramped quarters.

But they are where they belong,
in the bones of my home,
keeping it from collapsing and burying my body.

More will follow—
eyes to stare into rooms they reside in,
eyes to catch glimpses of their maker.

Ears to absorb wails and whimpers,
ears to trap hollow echoes of solitude.

Mouths to twist and curve in the direction I give them,
lips downturned more often
than not.

Stimulation

Muted television,
images blurred,
sharp movements
of indistinguishable shapes.

The couch's left cushion,
leather cracked from use,
soft,
dipping under her weight.

The wicks of Summer Moon
burn wax into a pool;
the house is damp grass
from heaps of humidity.

Christmas lights trace the window
year-round,
glinting in the corner of her eye.
She knows the order of the colors now.

White noise,
a machine bought to save the HVAC,
and a packet of bubblegum,
three sticks to replace the one in her mouth.

Only then,
when all is melded into mush,
is her head silent.

Reborn

I am lost in the stomach of the forest.
The trees have taken me,
shielding me from my life before.

Branches cradle my head
and pull me
into their spiny embrace.

Leaves form a covering
as the trickle of the river
lulls me into a dreamy haze.

A seed is placed inside my mouth
and I choke on it,
spit it up,

but they are persistent,
and soon I will become
one of them.

Finger Painting

My teeth belong to the desperate artist,
stripping back layers of my cuticles,
biting down on dry, hardened lips
to open vertical canyons,
gnawing at the ragged scabs of unhealed wounds
to create a palette with which
I will ravage our pristine walls.
A mural depicting everything you rejected,
everything you refused to see.

Still In Me

I withstand nights
where you wiggle into my mind.

I loved your hair, you know—
How the breeze combed through flaxen strands
as you passed me by,

and the scruff littering your jawline
that damaged my skin
wherever you forced a vengeful mouth.

Your arms,
built of well-trained muscle,
had their ridges and valleys

defined by streaks of motor oil
smeared across my skin
when you handled me.

Your towering body
would back me into a corner,
curling round me like a cocoon—
the looming, consuming protector.

I think no man protects
what he does not love.

Numbness

Fear the day of feeling nothing,
for it is cold and bare
and terribly lonely.
A day worth weeping for,
if you could.

Ritual

I take off my flesh and blood
and face and hair
at the end of my days,
and hang the suit in the closet
beside the others,
so my bones can stretch wide
and air themselves out,
loosening in preparation
for whomever I decide to wear
tomorrow.

Dad

I did not like the fruit punch in my cup,
so I dumped it out in front of the house;
red bled into the snow,
one large splash spreading,
scattered droplets
that made me panic
and run inside.
Toes tapping, I boiled water—
forgot to wear mitts to take the glass outside—
to pour on the stain.
Not enough.
Ten more trips before there was a hole
down to dead weeds,
and I could breathe a sigh of relief.
No one would think the crazy man
killed someone.

Mutilated

When they put your heart inside your body,
they gave no guarantee it will remain the same,
the same lovely shape,
the same perfect size.
They do not tell you what it will endure.
They do not warn of the choices you will make,
how the mistakes and heartbreaks
that will alter its form
into an unrecognizable state.

Kellam Road

Nestled in the field of green,
blades tall as they stretch
toward the summer sun,
butterflies come by
to kiss the tip of my nose.

Their legs perch with confidence
as beady eyes bore into mine,
wings spread wide,
steady to the breeze.

How naive they are,
how very unaware of my power
should I choose to abuse it;
too trusting.
I will not flick them away
with oily fingertips
or lure them into Mother's glass jars.

How lucky they are to fly,
to escape
before my whim shifts with the breeze
and I do my damage.

Alone

My voice is the only one I hear,
and I think
I am the only one to hear it,
as I invite no one else
to do so with me;

and with my voice,
I am loud, funny.
I say the things I would not say elsewhere.
I narrate stories as I write them.
I cry with my delivery of dramatic speeches
meant for those who will never hear them,
but those who should hear them most.

With my voice,
I am brilliant, sought-after;
I am on talk shows, answering questions;
on television shows, cultivating fans.
I am important, by myself,
creating strings of words
that will not be excised from my solitude.

But, sometimes,
I am afraid I am not alone,
that you are nearby, unseen,
as only you can be,
bearing witness to my antics.

I hope if you laugh,
it is with your child, and not at,
and you think me clever, witty, wonderful,
worthy of an audience's attention,
though I was unworthy of yours.

But it is likely
you watch with uncertainty
as to the stability of my sanity—
maybe caring enough to wonder
if I am like this
because you were never here.

Candy Jar

There was a jar,
bulbous and see-through,
whose lid your shaky hands should have dropped
but never did,
that you removed with each dive for a treat,
and replaced to trap the rest.

Trembling fingers untwisted cellophane wrappers,
crinkly, grating on the ears,
before you tossed them into a mass grave,
a pile stacking taller by the day.

You popped the sweets between stained lips,
and violently crunched with worn teeth,
swallowing what did not get stuck
in your cavities.

Trembling, shaking, repetitive—
crunch, swallow, lid ...
crunch, swallow, lid ...

I watched, mesmerized,
as your tongue turned muddy green,
and wondered what color I made
when you bit down on me.

Warning For All

I watched him crush and crumble
my body, he did break
and burn.
My ashes he sprinkled
over my least favorite places.

Fury

Above heads, wind whips,
knotting hair as sky cracks open
and pours warning shocks
into the Earth.

She cleaves in two,
and bits and pieces of our world
soar before our eyes
as rain attempts to drown us
and mud works to devour our shoes.

Home exists no longer;
our foundation has crumbled,
our wooden paneling has splintered,
our door cannot close
for waves of water.

And from your inability
to hold it all together—
your loss of control—
I take a moment to care about me
before you,
my pain over yours,
my wrath—
a formidable opponent to what you've harbored—
and my fury,
which shames the storm.

Feel It

Feel it all.

Feel its intensity.

Feel its rage,

feel its depth,

and feel its ache.

Feel it thoroughly.

Feel it now.

And hope it won't come for you

later.

Don't Cry For Me

She wonders if Death weeps
for those with no hope in their eyes—
the ones He takes before their time;
if He wipes away his tears
with bony fingers,
or if, when they meet,
she will have to do it for Him.

Flattened

He liked pressed flowers.
He would pluck them while they were fresh.
A daisy from under a suckling bee;
a tulip from the park where a girl skinned her knee,
flushed face, budding tears, pleading for her mother;
a rose from a funeral of a man he did not know;
a lily from the wedding of a couple he believed would not last,
and didn't.
He would take them home,
place them in a book,
and let the pages squeeze the life from them.

Mementos, I realized,
for the starved bee,
the harmed girl,
the dead man,
the broken couple.
I left him then,
before he could pluck and press a flower for me.

After Months

I will go out today,
escape the confines of my self-made cube,
witness the movements of other humans,
eat enough to fill my stomach,
breathe air not stale from circulation,
speak to someone other than the voice in my head,
try a little bit harder to live.

Trap

Do not chase what stands before you.

That which dares is much too eager—

much too willing to be caught.

You Can Have Her

Funny how I changed after us;
how I lopped my hair off,
dyed it blue,
and shed dry, cracked skin
for the soft and new.

Funny that with your departure,
you kept the old me with you,
as if she were not strong,
not brave enough to continue.

To Ash

I spent many years on fire
without seeing just how so.

Unknowingly sizzling,
secretly burning,

until it was only char
that made me.

Knock

It was too long before I realized:
I do not have to open the door
just because you stand
on the other side;
that your banging and pleading
does not have to mean to me
what you demand that it mean.
Let your knuckles bleed
on the front door of my house,
wait until you wither,
shout—
I hear you
for now,
but one day,
your squawks will blend with the birds.

To Look Back

Only once free
did I finally see us;
the culmination of our brutal parts
splayed before me
in undeniable honesty.

Twenty-Seven and Three

When I visit her in that house,
she is smaller than I remember,
her hair blonder, curlier,
her limbs chubbier.

She skips through flowers
that are up to her knees,
the same ones
that barely graze my ankles;
flowers on a slope of grass
that is not a grand hill,
where two dozen yards of pier
are not the mile they'd seemed.

I glance around on her behalf,
searching for more than I remember,
but he is not there;
she is alone, unguarded,
exposed,

and I wish I could spare her the pain
of what is to come,
to guide her down a different path—
the one I did not take.

Headspace

Why
when you are near
do the dark and damaged
pieces of my mind
tremble uneasily?

Unrealistic

I wish I could promise him the world,
but he doesn't want the world,
he wants me,
and maybe that is worse,
maybe that is harder to give.

Ethereal

I have read of gods and goddesses
and angels who tread our land,
deities and divine spirits
defined by those who worship them,
and I have wondered what inspired devotion
to creatures so unlike ourselves.

But one look upon your face and figure
and I understand
the draw of the ethereal,
the acceptance of all your kind gives us—
and a willingness to forfeit
all you desire to take away.

Perspective

I know me—
familiar with my height
and all I see in the mirror,

every freckle, flaw,
dimple, scar
seared into memory.

But you are tall—
you tower—
looking down upon me
at an angle inaccessible
to my eye.

What do you see from up there?
Things I do not,
marrings I have not yet disguised;

a wayward hair,
multiple shades from my poor dye job,
patchiness from spots where my fingers tug?

When you kiss the top of my head,
is that what your lips press against?
If so, then what madness compels you to do it again?

I Am Happy

What a shame to be happy
for all the lost things
that become elusive with joy:
the pain,
the words for the pain,
the tears just below the surface.
I miss the angst.

Forget Your First

Trauma was my first—
my lover years before you.
I pray you do not come to hate me
for that.

Savior

The day I wanted to die,
more than any of the days before,
I did not,
because I was not so lost
that thoughts could not find me,
and so,
I thought of you.

Rot

I have been in the belly of Darkness,
and with such vile rejection,
Darkness spat me back up.
So I clawed my way into its crannies,
the orifices it could not reach,
and I festered,
spreading like rot,
until Darkness knew my sickness—
my invulnerable decay;
and I ask
that you do not have me do the same
to you.

Filled

He does not pull out—
never in these moments.
Pulling out means emptiness.
Pulling out means a void
where he is missing,
and I am left wanting,
and we do not do that here,
tangled as we are.
Here is where I want for nothing.
Here is where I am full.

Host

If I dared to slice you open,
a line crooked or straight

I know the earth would spill out of you.

The packed soil under your skin
would finally breathe.

It would sip at the sun
and soak in the rain, and soon,

buds would beg to bloom.

Roots would weave with veins,
stems would stand tall through parted flesh.

Petals would unravel in vivid color
in such contrast to your tone.

And so the insects would make their way.

Your body—

their home.

Home

Though you are mine,
others flock and surround you,
drawn to the joy you emanate,
unable to tear themselves away,

while I step aside to settle by the sea.

Your voice fades to the waves
that slide over damp and heavy grains
to lap at my toes, retreat,
and reach for me again.

One of the few things that comes back,
I think, then chuckle.
The waves and you—
masters of the rebound.

It's impossible to push either away
without preparing myself
for inevitable return,
so unshakably constant.

The waves will not go anywhere,
and,
as my skin still feels your tingling touch,
I know neither will you.

Acknowledgments

I would like to thank:

My kind and encouraging editor, Sage Taylor Kingsley.

My very patient cover designer, Euan Monaghan.

Rodney Hatfield, who guided me through the final steps of my self-publishing journey. Your knowledge and expertise kept my anxiety from running rampant.

My therapist and psychiatrist. You've both worked very hard to keep me sane over the years. I'm sorry I've made that such a challenge.

Lindsay Bernal, my poetry professor at UMD (Fall semester, 2021). You once told me to trust and celebrate the strangeness of my poetry, so I did.

And my mom...for everything.

About the Author

Lauren Marelli is a poet and writer from Annapolis, MD. She studied poetry and received a degree in English Language and Literature at the University of Maryland. At nineteen, after being diagnosed with bipolar disorder, she found the beautiful world of poetry and has not let go of it. She hopes her poems help people feel solidarity at times when it seems no one else can understand their pain. *Under Your Nails* is her debut poetry book.

www.ingramcontent.com/pod-product-compliance
Lightning Source LLC
Chambersburg PA
CBHW031253120626
46545CB00007B/2799